Uphill Training
for
Off-Road Runners

By

Keven Shevels

TRAIL GUIDES
publications

First published in Great Britain in 2006 by Trailguides Limited.
Second edition published in Great Britain in 2010 by Trailguides Limited.
www.trailguides.co.uk

ISBN 978-1-905444-41-0

Trailguides Limited
35 Carmel Road South
Darlington
Co Durham DL3 8DQ

Cover design by Steve Gustard.

Contents

1. Introduction

Think off-road running and the first thing that most runners think of is hills. Whether you do cross-country, trail, fell or orienteering, you'll get a slight shiver down the back when you think of running uphill.

However, hills needn't be the bogyman that runners fear. With a change in attitude, the correct conditioning and the use of the appropriate techniques, hills can be changed to become a very useful weapon in the runners armoury.

Read the book. Go out and practice. The only thing that you have in front of you is improvement.

2. Physical Aspects of Running Uphill

2.1 What happens when you run uphill

We all know that running uphill is uncomfortable and hurts but why does it.

The first point to make is that running is a weight lifting exercise, albeit, a fast moving one. During the running stride, the leg muscles lift the body's weight up and off the ground in a forward direction. When running uphill, in addition to the body's weight, the leg muscles have to fight gravity by lifting the body higher and further up the slope of the hill. This means that the leg muscles have to work harder than on a corresponding level run. This affects the runner in two ways:

1.   The extra strength needed to physically lift the runner higher up the slope, and

2.   The extra energy consumption to power this increased work commitment.

Strength

Simply put, running is basically a type of jumping exercise. The runner uses one leg to jump off the ground and propel themselves forward. Granted the distance covered is no-where near that of the long jumper but during the running stride, the body of the runner does break contact with the ground and becomes airborne.

Lifting the body weight off the ground requires an element of strength, but during normal running, because the intention of the jump is not to gain height but rather to move forward parallel to the ground, then the amount of strength required is far lower than that required by a high jumper. However when running uphill, on each stride the body is physically moved to a higher level and the jump starts to acquire a vertical element in addition to the horizontal one. The more a body has to be moved vertically, then the more strength is required.

Energy consumption

The extra strength needed to run uphill requires extra energy. Research has shown that when compared to level running, running up an incline of 6% (6 metres of vertical climb per 100 metres of level distance) will use 35% more energy. A steeper incline will use correspondingly more.

As the majority of runners know, the best racing times will be achieved by even pace or more precisely, as a result of a constant energy output. This means that oxygen intake has to remain level as does the lactate level within the muscle.

Uphill running creates a problem with lactate and oxygen intake. As we see above, running uphill requires more energy to power the muscles. In order to create this extra energy, the body requires an increased supply of oxygen via increased breathing rates.

If the runner is already running at a fast pace while on level ground, then breathing and heart rates are already close to the limit. Therefore the amount of extra oxygen available to create additional energy is relatively small. The result is that the body has to use anaerobic energy which pushes the runner into oxygen debt resulting in rising lactate levels within the muscles.

As the runner travels uphill they will slow as the body tries to maintain a constant energy output. However, in spite of the slowdown, oxygen uptake and heart rate still increase as does blood lactate. These large amounts of lactate accumulate and will remain relatively high for the duration of the race. This can have the effect of reducing running performance long after the hill has disappeared into the distance. The correct training and tactics can help reduce these lactate effects and improve overall race times.

For endurance runners, the energy source {or pathway} is aerobic metabolism where fat and carbohydrate are metabolised into fuel to power the muscles. This metabolism requires oxygen to power it, which in turn is provided by the blood circulation system. Because the exercise intensity is relatively low, compared to sprinting for example, the body provides enough oxygen to fully metabolise the fat and carbohydrate stores.

Problems arise for the endurance runner when exercise intensity rises to such a level that the body cannot provide enough oxygen to fully metabolise carbohydrate. The body then moves into the anaerobic or "without oxygen" system. This energy pathway does not fully breakdown carbohydrate but does provide a high level of energy for a small period of time. This is the main fuel source of middle-distance runners such as those competing in the 800 metres and 1500 metres.

Unfortunately for the endurance runner this process produces a by-product known as lactate. This lactate builds up in the muscles and as well as inducing muscle soreness, causes the muscles to tire and slow down. As lactate levels increase the runner cannot maintain the same level of exercise. At very high levels, the effect can be very extreme with the runner virtually reduced to a walk.

2.2 Conditioning the body for uphill running.

As we are all aware a properly conditioned body will make coping with anything the race might present that much easier.

The most obvious way of conditioning the body for uphill running is to quite literally run uphill. This can be done as part of a steady run or as a specific hill training session.

However, in addition to this the body can be given specific exercises in order to improve it's conditioning and more readily prepare it for when it meets the hills. These exercises fall into two areas, strength and suppleness.

1.   Strengthening exercises increase the leg strength of the runner. This will improve the runner's ability to run up hills smoothly and with less effort. It will also help adapt the muscles to fight the effects of lactate. Stronger muscles tire less easily than weak ones and have an increased endurance capacity.

2.   Suppleness is about increasing the flexibility of a muscle. Running uphill is a strength activity and one of the effects of a strength activity is to shorten those muscles involved in that activity. When a muscle is short and tight, it is more prone to tears and strains when it is asked to lengthen during exercise. Improving the flexibility of the muscle will allow it to be more adaptable and reduce it's chances of being injured.

Let's now look at these two areas in more detail.

2.2.1 Strength

Strength is a vital necessity for the off-road runner both to support and power the running motion. Most runners prefer to perform their strength work through running itself, with no specific strength-based exercise. However, this can be a mistake and all runners will benefit from including some specific exercises into their routine, in particular to give them additional strength for climbing.

The muscle groups that will give most benefit for uphill running are

1.   The buttocks.
2.   The quadriceps.

> Lactate tolerance training is involved in Section 4: Training Sessions for Improvement.

3. The calves.
4. Lower back and trunk.
5. Arms and shoulders.

The buttocks.
These are used to power the backward drive of the leg. Heavily used when running uphill.

The quadriceps.
The thigh muscles. Again heavily used to lift the body upwards as the runner moves uphill.

The calves.
Used to lift the body on to its toes during the push-off stage of the running action. Placed under considerable strain when running up steep slopes.

Lower back and trunk.
The lower back takes heavy strain during steep climbing. The abdominal muscles help support the lower back.

Arms and shoulders.
The uphill running style makes a greater use of the movement of the arms to help generate uphill running power. Well toned arms and shoulder muscles will help sustain this movement.

There are two methods of increasing strength and both can be built into an all-round strength regime.

Weight training.
Weight training involves the use of a weight to perform exercises that will improve strength. Weight training equipment can be used at gyms and health clubs. For the dedicated runner it is even possible to buy their own. However for this booklet I have deliberately used exercises that only require the runner's own body weight to perform. This is in order to make the exercises accessible to all. The one exception to this, is the hammer curl for which the use of a small dumbbell is required.

Squats
Strengthens both the buttocks and the quadriceps.
Best performed as a single-leg exercise to gain the most benefit of using your own bodyweight as the resistance. This will also more closely mimic the running action of having the whole bodyweight supported by one leg. Perform the exercise 10 times and then recover. The

recovery time will be the amount of time that it takes to perform the exercise with the alternative leg. After recovery repeat.

Warning. Only take the squat down so that the knee is at 90 degrees with the thigh, parallel to the floor. Do not sink below this.

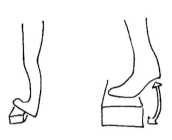

Toe lift.
Strengthens the calves.

Place the ball of the feet against something that will raise them 5 cm above the heels such as a block of wood (see diagram). Stand forward on the toes lifting the heels off the ground. This exercise can be done two-legged. Single-legged more accurately reflects the running motion and will provide the greater benefit. If doing one legged then a hand may be placed against a wall for support. Perform the lift 10 times and then recover. If doing one- legged., then the recovery will be the time that it takes to perform the exercise with the second leg. After recovery repeat the exercise.

Back raise.
Strengthens the lower back.

This exercise should be done slowly. Lay face down and keeping the hips on the ground, slowly raise the shoulders and arms off the ground. The training effect can be increased by holding the arms outstretched in front of the body. Perform the exercise 10 times and then recover. After recovery repeat. Recovery time will equal the time taken to perform the 10 reps.

WARNING. Only lift the top half of the body. Do not exaggerate the backward bending of the neck and back and bend too far.

Sit-ups
Strengthens the abdominals.

Using only the muscles of the abdominal, curl the body up to a position where the elbows touch the knees. Always perform sit-ups with the knees bent in order to avoid back injuries. Perform the exercise 10 times and then recover. After recovery repeat. Recovery time will equal the time taken to perform the 10 reps.

Hammer curls.
Strengthens the arms and shoulders.

A rarely used technique now but for the runner a very appropriate one as it

closely follows the arm movement of the running action. Similar to the biceps curl but instead of having the palm of the hand facing you, the hammer curl has the hand sideways.

Requires the use of dumbbells.

Hold the dumbbells down at the side of the body then alternatively raise each arm up from the elbow. Perform the lift 10 times with each arm and then recover. The recovery will be 50% of the time taken to perform the exercise. After recovery repeat.

So how does the heavily time-committed average runner fit a weights session into a hectic week's training schedule. One way is to replace an easy session with a weights session. Alternatively there is nothing to say that all the exercises need to be performed in one session. Try doing one exercise a day after your run has been completed. It will only add about 10/15 minutes to the length of the run. Use your common sense though, don't do any leg strength work on your quality training days. After a hard interval session you wouldn't want to do squats. Instead do one of the arm or trunk exercises.

Plyometrics

In "Downhill Techniques" the use of plyometrics was advocated for conditioning the body to the demands of downhill running. These same exercises, namely bounding and hopping, can also be used to condition the body for uphill running. They will improve the explosive eccentric strength, which is the force that provides the initial impetus as the runner takes-off on their stride. Instead of performing these exercises on level ground, simply do them upwards on a gently sloping hill.

Plyometrics sessions are a very intensive form of training but not only are they a good strength builder, they can seriously build your anaerobic fitness as well.

Initially if you have never done this type of exercise before, start with the first couple of sessions on a level field. Once you have become used to the technique and have developed a degree of eccentric strength,

Plyometrics are an extremely effective way of increasing eccentric strength. However they are also very intensive and because of the exaggerated foot strike they also multiply the impact shock. Because of this they should always be performed in well-cushioned shoes and on a soft surface. A level grassy field is ideal and never ever on concrete or tarmac. Female athletes should always be cautious about performing plyometrics in the week before their menstrual cycle as at this time they may be more susceptible to shin splints and stress fractures.

then you can move to doing the exercise up a shallow grass slope.

Bounding is simply an exaggerated running action. Push-off with the left foot and bring the leg forward with the knee bent and the thigh parallel to the ground. At the same time, reach forward with the right arm. As the left leg comes through, extend the right leg back and it is kept extended for the duration of the push-off. Hold the extended stride for a brief time before landing on the left foot. Repeat with the right leg. Make each stride long and try to cover as much distance as possible.

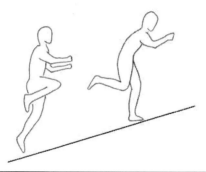

Single-leg hops. Push-off with the leg that you are standing on and jump forward landing on the same leg. Immediately take-off again and repeat until the required distance is covered or number of hops is completed. Try to cover as much distance as possible with each hop.

Uphill plyometrics should be performed on a gentle uphill slope of between 100 and 200 metres. Bound or hop the distance followed by a slow recovery walk back down to the start point and then repeat. Initially start with one or two reps and slowly build-up, adding an extra rep every couple of weeks.

For those new to this type of training then it will also be advisable to build-up slowly to the 100—200 metres distance by starting with ten bounds/hops and adding to it.

For the endurance runner it would be sufficient to perform this kind of exercise once a week. It could easily replace a steady run in the schedule.

One useful exercise that should not be under-estimated is quite simply walking up stairs. An easy-to-do exercise that is available to all except those that live in bungalows. This has the same movement pattern as steep climbing and will, therefore, train all the same muscle groups.

The exercise can be made into an even more effective one by carrying a weighted rucksack at the same time.

Number of reps for stair climbing. Start with 10 and add a rep each week. With a short distance and a steep gradient, most stairs can provide quite an intensive workout with or without the extra weight.

Very useful, especially to those who don't have ready access to the hills.

All exercises in this book either mobility, running or strength exercises should not be attempted without an adequate warm-up routine. Attempting any exercise "cold" before warming the muscles up sufficiently can lead to possible injury.

2.2.2 Suppleness

All runners should perform a regular stretching routine. The benefits are that obvious that I can't understand any runner that doesn't. Stretching will aid improved performance and help prevent injury. With regard to uphill running, the exercises that relate to the buttocks and the quads need particular focus. It is worth ensuring that the following exercises are included in your routine.

Stand on one leg. With one hand grasped around the ankle bring the non-supporting leg back until the heel touches the buttocks. Hold for 30 seconds. Feel the stretch in the quads. Repeat with the other leg.

Sit and place the left arm behind for support. Holding the right leg straight out, place the left foot on the outside of the right knee. Use the right elbow to gently push the left leg across the body. Hold the stretch for 30 seconds. Feel the stretch in the left hamstring and buttock. Repeat with the other side. As a secondary effect, this exercise also helps the trunk.

One other aspect that is often forgotten by off-road runners is the lower back and trunk. These take a lot more of a pounding than most people imagine especially on long uphills and can result in stiff and sore muscles the next day. Ensure that you include some flexibility exercises for these areas into your routine. Try the ones below.

Sit and slowly bend forward from the waist. Thread the arms through the legs and hold the ankles. Bring the head forward between the ankles and hold for 30 seconds. Feel the stretch in the lower back.

Kneel on all-fours. Arch the back similar to a cat's and hold for about 10/20 seconds. Relax and let the belly sag downwards for 10 seconds, then repeat. Feel the stretch in the back.

Kneel and with the arms sloping backwards, bring the head forward to between the knees. Hold for 30 seconds. Feel the stretch in the back.

Where possible, stretching exercises should be held for 30 seconds. If due to shortened muscles, you are unable to complete the full stretch movement then take it to the point where you just feel uncomfortable. **Never take a stretch to the point where it becomes painful.**

3. Technical Aspects of Running Uphill

3.1 Uphill techniques.

The general opinion from those not involved with off-road running is that you find a hill in front of you and you just run up it. For those of us who are involved, we know that it isn't that simple.

In this section we will look at the various techniques that can be used to improve your uphill running. These range from why you should plan your race, to more specific such as stride length. However they do all work and each is worthy of being considered in your search to improve your overall race performance.

Stable and Unstable Ground
In this guide the terms stable and unstable ground are often mentioned.

In order to make the most effective use of the running stride the runner needs to place his/her foot on a hard level surface. This will enable them to make the most use of their energy and power to push themselves away from the ground on the take-off stage off the stride. The classic examples of hard level running surface are athletics tracks and roads. These are considered to be stable surfaces.

In the off-road world nothing is as stable as these two, although such surfaces as forest roads and well-made vehicle tracks can be considered as stable. Any other ground will be considered as being unstable to various degrees because it does not allow the runner to make the maximum use of his/her energy and power.

This instability may be due to the ground being soft and absorbing energy or being uneven and/or loose and not allowing the runner to push-off in a straight line or it could be any combination of the two. Because of this, running on unstable ground is naturally slower than on stable ground.

For the off-road runner, the choice is finding the least unstable ground to run over in order to make the most effective use of his/her running action.

3.1.1 Planning

Very few runners plan their race. Most just leave the start line on the word "go" and run as the mood and feeling take them and this applies to road, trail and fell runners.

Unfortunately this attitude can affect your whole race performance. When it comes to trail and fell running, this can have an even more critical effect. Both trail and, in particular, fell races will contain longer and steeper hills than, say, a corresponding road race. Hillier courses have a much higher energy requirement to complete. As shown, previously compared to running on the level, running up an incline of 6% will use 35% more energy. However on the corresponding down hill the energy expenditure is only reduced by 24%.

> The length and steepness of the hills encountered during your race can become a crucial factor in your running endurance. Planning your race beforehand and deciding your pace and effort for each hill can be an advantage.

As you progress your way round the course encountering climbs and descents as you go then this will give you peaks and troughs of energy expenditure. Depending upon the course these may be quite severe.

Both trail and fell running are endurance based. This means that the best results come from even-paced running, or to be more accurate, even-paced energy expenditure. This then gives a basic contradiction with the nature of off-road running and it's energy requirement highs and lows.

As far as possible the nature of the route needs to be taken advantage of in order to lessen these peaks and troughs and produce a more uniform energy expenditure. Granted this will never produce a straight line expenditure but with a little bit of forethought it can be levelled out a bit.

This means that your race should be planned. Identify where these big highs and lows are going to come. Adapt your race strategy to take this into account, for

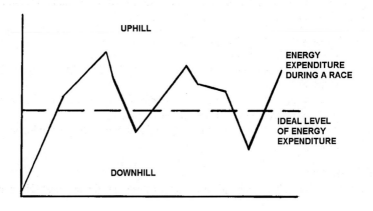

example, reduce the pace in the early uphills to conserve energy to meet demands later in the race.

This can be taken to an even lower level still, by planning for each individual hill. On a long steep climb towards the beginning of the race, you may decide to slow down your running pace in order to save energy and then attack a shorter, shallower hill later in the race when you judge that your competitors are starting to suffer.

However, this all takes knowledge of the route in order to prepare. You need to know where the uphills and downhills are, how steep they are and what the terrain is like. If you've done the race before then you should have this knowledge. If you haven't then you'll have to do some research or at least ask somebody who you know has completed the course. Either way there is always going to be an advantage in actually running over the race route a week or so before the event.

3.1.2 Route choice

Route choice is deciding which way to go. This can take two forms. With events that test navigation ability such as orienteering, Mountain Marathons and some fell races it is quite literally deciding do I go that way or do I go this way. On the majority of fell, trail and cross country races the route is given and marked for you to follow. In these cases the choice is restricted to which side of the track should I run on, where should I place myself for the climb etc. This is known as "taking a line". We will look at each of these in turn.

Route choice
In those events that include an element of route choice, there are several factors that need to be taken into consideration. Most of these fall outside the scope of this booklet. For further information see the sister booklets "Mountain Marathon Preparation" and "Navigation for Off-Road Runners".

However, factors that do come into play include:
1.   How long is the climb
2.   What is the nature of the ground underfoot, will I be able to run or will it force me to walk.
3.   How steep is the slope, again, will I be able to run or be forced to walk.
4.   Are there any potential hazards if I go off-route.
5.   Are there any alternatives that will be faster even if they are a longer distance.

Taking a line.
With taking a line, The basic rule is the shortest route is the quickest. The shortest

route normally being a straight line.

However, there are other factors that need to be taken into account. These factors are dependant on the principle that in order to run fast requires a good solid surface for the running step to take-off from. Soft and unstable ground surfaces force a slower running speed.

To a limited extent these decisions about taking a line can be made as you progress through the event but prior knowledge of the event and the route would be a great help in making these decisions. This goes back to the previous section on planning. A pre-race recce of the route and deciding what lines to take can save valuable time when it comes to the race.

Even when following a track upwards, a straighter-line route cutting the corners can save distance and time during a race. However, be aware that the gradient on the inside of a bend going uphill, is nearly always steeper than that on the outside of the bend.

Straight-line travel is not always faster. Rather it is dependant upon the running speed that can be maintained. In the situation left, provided that the slope is not too steep and running can be maintained, then running straight up would be faster.

However, if the slope were steeper, to the point where to go straight ahead would require walking, then the longer zig-zag route could be faster. The zig-zags would have a reduced gradient compared with the straight-line which would enable them to be run.

If the slope gets even steeper so that both the straight-line and the zig-zag approach required walking, then the straight-line would, once again, become faster.

Vegetation and the running surface may also become factors. Even if you can run through heather, bracken or tall grass, they may still slow you down sufficiently so that a longer distance on firmer, easier running ground is faster. The same may apply if the ground is soft or loose.

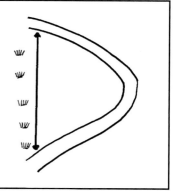

3.1.3 Balance

Not something that is immediately thought of as being required to improve your uphill technique. Indeed if you are still running up a slope then there is no additional need other than that required for level running. However, this changes as the slope gets steeper and especially as the slope gets steeper to the point where the runner has to resort to walking. At this point greater demands are placed on the runners ability to keep an upright posture and forward momentum.

More than one of us will have had the situation where as we are struggling to push our bodies forward and upwards, just for a moment we lose the forward momentum and for a few seconds are stood there on the one-leg and off-balance. At best this can cause lost time, at worst, being off-balance can either cause the foot to slip or a forward fall into the hill and sometimes even both.

A more developed sense of balance wouldn't eliminate the possibility of this happening but can reduce the occurrences and help maintain forward momentum.

Exercises

For those that have read "Downhill techniques" you'll find the same balancing exercises below. No apologies for repeating them. They are effective and they work, so why re-invent the wheel.

One that comes from the race walking fraternity is that of walking along a line with the feet going heel to toes. Very similar to the test to see whether you are drunk or not. As you walk, swing both arms round in wide circles. Sounds crazy but it works otherwise the race walkers wouldn't do it. This can be built-in to your warm-up routine either as part of a running session or a circuit training session.

Another example is using a wobble-board for a balance exercise. These are often used during rehabilitation from injury but can be used as a training aid in their own right. This also has the added benefit of strengthening the ankles.

If you don't fancy the expense of or don't have access to a wobble-board, an alternative exercise is to stand on one leg with your arms out, slightly bend the knee and then close your eyes. Now try and stand like that for 30 seconds without falling over. Repeat a couple of times a day. Again, this also has the added benefit of strengthening the ankles.

And last but not least. Have a go at tight-rope walking. Set a rope up just above the ground or use a narrow plank of wood and walk along it. It's surprising how effective this can be in developing a sense of balance. Not surprising but this is an exercise often used by climbers.

As extra curriculum activities to running, any of the board sports such as skateboarding, surfing or snowboarding will all help to develop balance.

3.1.4 Angle of lean

Those of you who have read the sister booklet "Downhill Techniques" will know about the importance of the angle of lean in running downhill but how can it be used when running uphill.

The angle of lean is the amount that the runner leans forward from the hip while running.

Running uphill is very stressful and demands a great deal of strength. The muscles that produce the majority of that strength are the buttock muscles. They provide the

When leaning forward into the hill it is important to keep the buttocks under you. Try and keep them tucked in line with the body to ensure the maximum usage of this major muscle group.
Leaning too far forward can cause the runner's bottom to stick-out and push them away from the line of the body reducing their effectiveness.

powerful backward drive of the legs that propel you forward, and, in the case of hill climbing, upwards.

The force produced by these buttock muscles can be multiplied by leaning the body forward from the hip. This increases the effective length of the muscle thus generating more force.

Therefore leaning into the hill gives greater strength to power up the hills. How far forward you lean and how much power you need to run up the hills will depend upon the length of the hill. The cross-country runner faced with a 400 or 600 metre hill, even of a relatively steep gradient, will be capable of powering up the hill and would therefore gain most benefit from a higher angle of lean. With a hill that has any length, then economy of effort becomes the deciding factor. Powering your way uphill is very energy costly, therefore, with a long hill the emphasis is more on conserving energy and so there is less need for power and the angle of lean would be much reduced to the point where it would be just slightly forward of the vertical.

However no matter how reduced the angle of lean is, it is crucial to maintain some degree of forward lean. Forward lean ensures forward momentum. As soon as this lean disappears and the body becomes vertical, forward momentum is lost and the runner immediately starts to lose pace and on a steep slope can even come to a standstill.

This angle of lean principle applies even when the runner has been reduced to walking due to the steepness of the slope. In fact, it may even be more important as, if the slope is that steep that the runner is reduced to walking, putting the body into the vertical upright position instead of the forward lean, may bring the forward and upwards momentum to a complete halt.

During the course of a race, different lengths and angles of hills may be encountered. In this case the angle of lean would be changing to suit each individual slope and the runner's own race plan. This is part of the importance of planning as discussed earlier.

Is there any possible problems with this angle of lean principle. Well yes there are:
1. Leaning too far forward can upset the body's centre of gravity and cause the runner to stumble and/or fall into the hill.
2. Leaning too far forward does have the potential to constrict the body's breathing thus restricting oxygen intake.

Leaning forward works by throwing the bodyweight to the front. An upright position tends to throw the weight back thus reducing forward momentum and even causing backwards movement in extreme cases.

Exercise

What is required from the runner is a little bit of experimentation and doing some up-hill running tests and varying the forward lean. Learn how it affects your uphill running, how you can control it and how far forward you can and need to lean. Perform a series of short hill reps. The emphasis will not be on speed or strength but rather experience. As you run uphill lean further into and then back out of the hill. Notice the effect that it has on your running. Try this on different types of gradient.

Leaning into the hill helps ensure forward momentum. This applies when both running and walking.

3.1.5 Stride length.

As with downhill running, getting the correct stride length to suit the angle of the hill is a vital skill that needs to be learnt. Failure to gauge the length correctly will result in high lactate levels, tight leg muscles and very rapid breathing. This, in turn, will result in a severe drop in pace, enforced walking and quite often "standing to look at the scenery".

So what is the correct stride length for uphill running. The answer to that is determined by the hill itself. The steepness and the length of the hill will dictate the necessary stride.

On shallower hills it is possible to reduce the stride by only a small amount. Steeper hills will require a much shorter stride. In many cases the hill wouldn't allow you to over stride and it is extremely difficult to maintain the same stride length as you have been using on the flat. As the hill steepens keep reducing the stride length. In extreme cases this may result in a motion very similar to walking upstairs. If the gradient decreases then you will find it possible to extend the stride again.

The stride length itself must be shortened at the foot of the hill. Even on shallow hills maintaining your normal stride part way up the hill will result in increased effort and lactate rates.

Indications that your stride length is too long are
1.   Breathing too rapidly.
2.   Tight hamstrings.
3.   Sore shins.

Maintaining a smooth, even breathing pattern is a good measure of appropriate stride length.

Another factor that needs to be considered when thinking about stride length is the length of the hill. As we have seen, running uphill consumes considerable amounts of energy and a long uphill will obviously consume more than a short uphill. Economy of effort then becomes the name of the game.

A shorter stride length is more economical and on long slopes reducing the stride length has advantages in the longer term, even though on the same gradient but with a shorter distance you could comfortably maintain a longer length.

Exercise
Perform a series of hill reps on a climb that has a number of variations in slope angle/gradient. Practise changing your stride length as you run up.

3.1.6 Foot plant

Planting the foot on the ground during uphill running has two aspects:
1.   Positioning the foot, and
2.   Using a ball of the foot or whole sole foot plant.

Positioning.
Most shallower ascents tend to have a more stable and sound running surface. Steeper climbs, due to the angle of the hill, will have a rougher and more unstable surface. When planted on an unstable surface, as the foot presses down, either the ground can give way or the foot can move on the loose surface and produce a backwards slip. This can produce a loss in forward momentum and potentially lost time and/or a fall. It is always advisable to try and pick your step position as you climb. While this technique wouldn't make you any faster, failure to pay attention to it will make you slower.

Ball or whole sole foot plant.
On shallower ascents the runner's natural running style can be maintained whether it is toe first or heel first. But as the climbs get steeper the tendency is to move towards a toe first, or more accurately the ball of the foot,

> As the gradient of the hill becomes steeper, the runner will naturally move towards planting the foot on the ball of the foot.

23

foot plant. Bear in mind that on a steep climb, if you plant the whole foot on the ground then the heel is going to be below the level of the ball of the foot. This will put the calf muscle under strain and could potentially lead to injury, at the least it would lead to sore calves. The strain can also quickly tire the calf muscles with a resulting drop in running pace.

It is advisable to counter this with a little bit of mix and match. Keep on the balls of the feet for the majority of the climb and then every so often, when the gradient permits, do a full foot plant for a short distance. This relieves some of the strain from running on the front of the foot and uses the fact that the heel is below the front of the foot to stretch the calf a bit while you run.

3.1.7 Stamina-lactate build up

As we have seen in "Section 2: What happens when you run uphill", the accumulation of lactate in the leg muscles can have a severe effect on the body's ability to run and for the off-road runner, uphill running is the biggest generator of lactate.

There are two ways of combating this:
1.   Reducing the amount of lactate within the muscles, and
2.   Improving the body's ability to tolerate lactate.

Reducing the amount of lactate within the muscles.
Unfortunately it's not possible to defy the laws of nature and totally stop producing lactate, so how can you reduce the amount swilling around the muscles ?

First off, you need to understand that as well as being produced by the metabolism of fuel into energy, lactate itself can also be used as a fuel and so taken back out of the body. Unfortunately it is a rather poor quality fuel compared to carbohydrate and even fat. It is slow to convert and the body will produce it faster than it can be used which is what leads to the build-up in the muscles.

By controlling your running pace it is possible to reach an equilibrium point where the amount of lactate being used is equal to that being created. Slowing the running pace down as you run uphill will ensure that your muscles do not become saturated with lactate.

This all comes down to pace control and being able to determine the effects of your running speed on your body. Unfortunately this only comes through experience but it is possible to speed up gaining this experience by utilising a heart rate monitor as you run. This would enable the effects of different running paces to be felt and judged.

Improving the body's ability to tolerate lactate.

It is possible to train the body to become more tolerant of lactate. In essence, to perform with a higher level of lactate within the muscles.

As work rate/energy output goes up then so does the volume of lactate in the muscles. When this exceeds the body's tolerance level then performance will deteriorate. Tolerance or threshold training, as it is commonly called, is designed to accustom the body to running with a higher level of lactate in the muscles than the current tolerance level. By regularly repeating this exercise, the body will then slowly raise the tolerance level enabling a higher standard of performance.

The knack to these sessions is to generate enough lactate to slightly exceed tolerance but not too much where the excess gets that high that it prevents running. Pace and/or heart rate needs to be carefully monitored throughout the session.

As with all training this involves putting the body under a little stress and then waiting for it to adapt before putting it under a little more. In this case this involves running at a fast enough pace to generate an excess of lactate but not too fast where the excess gets that high that it prevents running. Regular training at this pace accustoms the body to performing with a higher level of lactate within the muscles.

As the body becomes more accustomed to working at this level of effort, you will notice that the running pace will get faster while the heart rate will remain at a constant intensity.

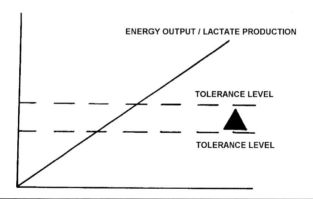

The principle of tolerance or threshold training is to raise the tolerance level enabling the body to perform with an increased level of lactate within the muscles without pushing it past the point where performance deterioration starts to occur.

Actual tolerance/threshold training sessions are discussed on page 43 including the relevant use of heart rate monitors.

3.1.8 Transition

Transition is that moment when the movement changes from one type to another. Every climb involves two transitions, one at the start of the climb and one at the end. With uphill running this can happen in four ways.

1. The transition from running on the level to running uphill.
2. The transition from running downhill to running uphill.
3. The transition from running uphill to running on the level, for example running up and onto a summit plateau.
4. The transition from running uphill to running downhill is a more specific downhill exercise and is covered in the "Downhill Techniques" book.

From level running to uphill.
The most common form of transition is that from level to uphill. As discussed previously the most effective way of running up a hill is to shorten the stride length and slow the speed down. Most runners wait until the last moment to change down a gear in order to get the maximum benefit from the longer stride length being used while running on the level. However, delay the changeover too long and you run the risk of over- striding on the uphill. This will have the effect of over- stretching the leg muscles and starting the build-up of lactate prematurely. The change of stride length needs to occur just at the point where the level ground changes to the uphill slope. However, this is not always easy to do and it is quite often difficult to even identify where this point is on the hill. To be able to judge this requires practice and not just practise on the one hill, as all hills have different angles of gradient. The runner will need to practise on a range of different slopes and gradients.

Exercise
Perform a series of hill reps starting 300/400 metres before the base of the hill. Before the first rep, walk the hill and estimate where the change over point would be. Perform the reps using this change over point and judge the effect on your legs and stamina. It would also be worthwhile performing a few reps where you change stride length 50 metres too early and 50 metres too late. Notice the effect that an error in judgement can have.

From downhill running to uphill.
Probably the biggest shock to the system is when you run downhill and then immediately have to start running uphill straight away. This usually happens when

you are crossing small valleys, down one side, cross a small stream and straight back up the other side with no real flat area at the bottom. Normally in these situations both the descent and the climb are quite steep as shallow sided valleys tend to have an extended valley floor.

In most cases, this sudden change in movement pattern tends to make the runner resort to walking up the hill. This is partially due to the physical aspect of suddenly changing the work rate and the movement patterns of the muscles in the legs but also the physiological effect of the sudden change from relatively easy work downhill to a hard uphill effort. Yet again, the only way to really prepare for this is to practice.

Exercise
Perform a series of reps in a steep sided valley where you can run down and then straight back up again. The distance of the reps, including both down and up sections, should be between 600 to 800 metres. Run down and then up. At the end of the rep take a recovery before repeating the rep in reverse to get back to your starting point. This would be classed as two reps. Perform a series of 10 to 12 reps.
The recovery should be between 50% to 100% of your running time dependant upon fitness. If you have to walk the uphill, then still do the reps. The session is designed to replicate actual race conditions and to condition the body for the change from going down to going up.

From uphill running to on the level.
The situation happens more often than people realise either through running to the top of a hill and then over a summit plateau or just running part-way up a hill and then more horizontally for a period of time.
The change from the stresses of running uphill to all of a sudden, the relatively reduced stress of level running can be a shock to the legs especially after a long steep climb that has involved uphill walking. Most runners will continue walking over the top of the hill for some distance in order to recover from the uphill. Obviously the sooner you can start running again, the more benefit this will be to your race time but this will depend upon your fitness and how conditioned your body is to start running straight after a steep uphill.

Exercise
Perform a series of hill reps on a steep incline. If possible one where it is necessary to walk in the upper section. Instead of turning round at the top, extend the rep by 300/400 metres of level running. As you hit the top of the climb start to run immediately to complete the additional 300/400 metres.

One area that should not be neglected is those situations where on a long uphill the gradient is constantly changing and the angle of slope will vary from steep to shallow and all shades in-between. This may give you sections of the climb where your pace will change as you try to take maximum advantage of all running opportunities. Try and build into your training, sessions on hills with variable slopes such as this and practise pace changing as you run. Try to learn how to maximise the amount of running that you can get out of a particular slope.

3.1.9 Warming-up

Cast your mind back to the beginning of this booklet and "Section 2: What happens when you run uphill". There we discussed high exercise intensity, anaerobic energy and lactate. Now we look at these effects on the start of a race.

At the start of any exercise, irrespective of how intense it is, the energy supply will always be anaerobic. This is because it takes a couple of minutes before the body's aerobic system starts to function fully. That is before breathing rate, heart rate and the transport of oxygen through the blood adjust to the demands of the activity.

The consequence of this is that right from the start of a run the body is building up lactate. Normally for the endurance runner, as they get into their stride and the aerobic energy system comes into play, this "start up" lactate is dissipated and has no long-term effects on race performance.

However, many trail runs and virtually all fell runs have a hill of some degree close to the start. This gives the situation where the runner is accumulating lactate from the start of the race and before that is being dispersed, they are then moving into an intensive exercise period that is going to generate even higher additional amounts of lactate on top of that already in the system. It's no wonder that the start of a race can be so painful and can effect your performance over the whole run.

So how can the effects of this be reduced. The easiest and most beneficial is to do an adequate warm-up before the start of the race. This will mean that the body's initial anaerobic start-up phase will have passed and the lactate mostly dispersed before the competitive running begins. In addition, it will also move the runner into the aerobic phase of running before the intensive hill climbing starts which, in turn, will delay the start of the lactate build-up caused by the hill climb.

The warm-up routines performed should consist of easy jogging leading into faster but still easy paced running. Dynamic stretching and flexibility exercises can also be built into the routine. The intention is to raise the body temperature to just above the normal core temperature of around 37c (98f). This needs to be reached within ten minutes of the race starting. The increased body temperature will also improve blood circulation and the oxygen transport system within it. Muscle elasticity will also be improved which permits a greater range of joint movement.

While the better quality runners normally do the full warm-up, the average runner tends to just pay lip service to the principle. This is a mistake and all off-road runners, irrespective of their ability, will improve their performance from doing just a simple thing as an adequate warm-up before the start of the race.

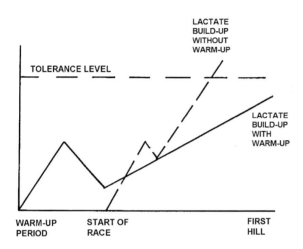

3.1.10 Walking

Not something that is normally considered in any other running discipline but in both trail and fell running the ability to walk positively is a downright advantage. In many races there are sections of the route where the uphill climb is just too long and steep that running becomes more inefficient than walking up the hill.

Done correctly fast, positive walking can actually get you to the top of the hill faster than running and in a more energy efficient manner. Most runners when they reach the walking stage, subconsciously throttle back, stand upright and more passively walk uphill. However, if instead they follow all the same rules that relate to running uphill such as stride length, angle of lean, arm movement, foot plant, etc, then they will find that their climbing times will reduce.

When walking steeply uphill it is also possible to use the hands to take some of the load off the over-worked legs. See the section on hands.

So how do you know when to stop running and start walking. Basically at some point on a climb this will be forced on you and you will know when you can't run any further. At this point you have gone too far, the walking should have started slightly before this, just before you have gone into over-load. This needs to be practised so that the runner can recognise this point easily in the heat of competition. See the exercise below.

Don't underestimate the effectiveness of walking. I've ran against people who walk virtually all of the uphills as I've ran past them. The same people have been waiting for me at the finishing line. They were more effective than me at planning their race and being energy economical on the uphills through walking. The result was that I was well and truly stuffed by those runners.

Exercise.
Perform a series of hill reps on a slope where the gradient will force you to walk. Try to identify the point before the over-load forces you to start the walking. At the same time practise using your hands to help you climb. Try to build up a portfolio of different slopes and terrain that you have to walk up.

> When walking uphill, it is critical to maintain the forward lean and, as much as possible, the arm swing, otherwise what is a competitive activity becomes merely a stroll.

3.1.11 Hands

Sounds strange using the hands for a running activity but for the off-road runner there are times when the use of your hands can be very beneficial.

The hands can be used in two ways, both of which occur when the climb has become so steep that the runner is reduced to walking.

When using the hands to take some of the strain off the legs it is crucial to get the placement of the hands correct. The position should be over the knee and not the midpoint of the thigh. See illustration on back cover.

The first method is using the hands to help assist the legs to raise the body weight by placing the hands on the legs and pushing down as you stride. The principle of this manoeuvre is that the force pushing downwards by the hands through the tibia and fibula will react with an equal force that allows the upper part of the body to be levered up just for a second. This helps take the full strain of lifting the body away from the legs. You wouldn't automatically feel the effect of this technique but over a long prolonged climb it can make a major contribution to saving energy.

However, when using this technique it is crucial to get the placement of the hands correct. The mistake made by most runners is in the placing of the hands on the mid-point of the thigh. Any downward pressure at this point stops the quads from straightening the legs and will actually restrict the climbing ability.

Instead the hand should be placed lower down so that the heel of the hand is just above the knee with the thumb on the inside of the knee, the index finger over the knee and the middle finger on the outside of the knee. The downward push from the hand has to be timed to coincide with the lifting motion of the leg. The downward pressure from the hand should be applied just for a moment. Too long and it will take away any advantage gained. When released the hand should remain close to the knee ready for the next move.

The second method of using the hands comes into play when the slope becomes even steeper and rougher. On very steep climbs, it is possible to haul yourself up by using heather and other vegetation, rock outcrops and any object that comes to hand. Using the hands in this way can help take some of the pressure off the legs and give some relief from the lactate build-up.

3.1.12 Arms

Not really considered much by the average runner, the arms are a vital part of the running motion. However, with the endurance off-road runner they do tend to be

Cross-body arm
movement

Backwards and forwards arm
movement

used in the passive sense.

When running on the level they tend to follow the classic endurance runner's style of close to the side and moving backwards and forward, slightly across the body. In essence providing a counter-balance to the movement of the legs. When descending they can be raised out from the side to aid balance and increase stability but again this is more of a passive movement.

Now watch a sprinter in action and you'll see the arms being pumped strongly in a backwards and forwards movement. They do not cross the body but move parallel to the plane of motion.

This movement helps the sprinter produce the power to travel short distances very fast. A similar movement can be adopted by the trail and fell runner to assist them in running up hills. At the approach to the bottom of the hill change the arm movement from moving across the body to a more dynamic backwards and forwards movement.

Adopt a higher and more
powerful arm swing for
shorter length hills i.e.
cross-country.

With a lower, more
economical arm swing for
longer length climbs i.e.
climbs of a mile and above.

In terms of movement, the legs will follow the arms and this change in movement pattern aids momentum quite significantly on an upwards slope. To illustrate this point try the following exercise.

Exercise

Go for a run and for a short distance try and run with your arms straight down, hanging by your side. You will find that the movement of your legs is restricted as is your ability to run comfortably. Now try running with the arms moving as normal slightly across the body. Much more freedom of movement for the legs and more comfortable. Finally try moving the arms backwards and forwards instead of across the body. You'll see your momentum increase without any conscious change in effort by yourself. Pump your arms harder and higher until they reach near to the ear.

Right, so if pumping the arms backwards and forwards helps momentum so much, then why doesn't the runner do it all the time. The answer to that is because it is so energy expensive compared to the cross-body swing. During normal endurance running it is more beneficial not to do it. However, running uphill is, itself, so energy costly that the situation changes and it becomes much more essential to maintain forward momentum than to save that additional energy that the forward swing costs.

But as always nothing is as cut and dried as all that. To maintain a powerful backwards and forwards arm swing over a long steady climb takes well conditioned arm and shoulder muscles. Even top flight runners would have problems over such long climbs as Snowdon and the Ben. So in reality what happens is a bit of a compromise.

The longer the hill, then the more the arm action is minimised with a shorter backwards and forwards swing. The reverse also applies, the shorter the hill, the more powerfully the runner can attack it and the arm swing becomes more pronounced. Note that during the minimised swing the arms never revert back to the cross-body style but retain the backwards and forwards motion just with a reduced height of swing.

Once the climbing has finished, the runner can return to the more economical cross-body style of arm swing.

Arm swing can be adapted anywhere between high and low to suit the hill length that you are running up. This is where knowledge of the route and race planning come into help determine the most effective running style.

3.1.13 Running with a rucksack

There are some aspects of off-road running such as Mountain Marathons that require the carrying of a rucksack. As you would expect, carrying an additional load will require additional energy consumption compared to running without one.

If the runner is travelling at the same pace with a load as when they are without, then they are already working higher-up the intensity scale before they even approach the hill. As they are already working at this high intensity, then the accumulation of lactate will begin much sooner than running with no load.

The runner needs to be aware of this and make corresponding changes to race planning and pacing. Regular pre-event training sessions should include carrying the full kit in order for both the body and the mind to make these adaptations.

> Running with a rucksack effectively increases your bodyweight. When running uphill this gives a requirement for extra strength and increases your work rate thus speeding-up lactate overload. This means that careful attention needs to be given to pace judgement. A slower running speed will need to be used to maintain acceptable levels of lactate within the muscles.

3.1.14 Bodyweight

As a sixteen stone, malnourished beanpole myself, this is one area that I do hate to mention but it is something that does have an effect on climbing ability and does merit being included. The average runner will read and take no-notice but even the loss of a single pound will bring some degree of improvement.

Running uphill is a strength activity. The runner lifts their own body weight up the hill using their leg strength. How effectively the runner does this is judged by their strength to weight ratio. The higher their strength compared to their weight, then the easier and faster it will be to climb those hills.

So how can this strength/weight ratio be improved. One obvious way is to increase strength, see "Section 2: Conditioning the body for uphill running". The next option is to lower weight. Reducing weight while maintaining leg strength will automatically improve the strength/weight ratio.

Elite athletes normally have a body fat content of under 10% for men and under 15% for women. While not suggesting that every runner should reduce to these sort of levels, we all have maybe a pound or two that we could lose.

One other factor that needs to borne in mind is that of body and size and energy expenditure. If all other factors such as fitness level and percentage body fat are equal, then the runner who is smaller in stature will expend less energy while running uphill than the larger runner. Therefore, running uphill is, relatively easier for the smaller person. The larger person becomes more energy efficient when running over level ground.

Granted that we cannot change our body size other than a little bit of weight loss, then how can this knowledge affect our race performance. Well, it can affect our planning and the way that we approach the uphills.

For the larger runner, approach the uphills in a more energy conservative manner. Try and take them in a more even expenditure style and slow the pace down. Don't view every section of the race as competitively, be prepared to let some runners pull away from you on the uphill knowing that the advantage will change to you when the slope levels out.

For the smaller runner, take advantage of those sections of the course that nature has given you the edge on. Use the hills, try and open gaps between you and your competitors. Try and get as big an advantage as you can on the uphills, this will be whittled back once you are back to level running.

3.2 Mental attitude

Most runners don't like hills, they see hills and think of pain and suffering. The off-road runner can't afford the luxury of this attitude. Hills are a fundamental part of what the trail and fell runner loves, running in the great outdoors.

A positive mental attitude towards hills is a must. The runner has to know that they have the physical capability and technique to rise above the hill (and yes, the pun was intended). The best way to develop this attitude is through training and this has to be consistent training. Use hills that are similar to those you expect to meet in racing. Train on them, practise the techniques, develop the strength and pace judgment. In short, take away that fear. And develop a mental toughness towards hills.

When you line-up on the start knowing that you have done all this in training, then just the sheer confidence in your own ability will improve your race performance.

4. Training Sessions for Improvement

4.1 Constructing an uphill running session

As we have seen there are two component parts to improving your uphill running.
1. Improving your uphill running strength.
2. Improving your lactate tolerance.

However, bear in mind that these two are not mutually exclusive. Dependant upon the chosen training session it is possible to combine the two.

4.2 Improving your uphill running strength.

This is normally done by performing a version of hill rep. There are three ways of incorporating hill reps into your training.

1. Uphill reps. The type of session normally regarded as the classic hill rep session. Running hard uphill with an easy jog back down to the start as a recovery. These can be done as reps of an equal distance or as a pyramid session.

2. Up and downhill reps. A variation on the normal hill reps but instead of taking a recovery on the way back down, the effort is continued on the downhill after the climb. The recovery being taken as a rest before starting the next hill. This form of session is particularly useful if training for a shortish straight up and down race as it gets the body accustomed to hard effort immediately turning into a flat out descent.

3. Structured Fartlek. A structured fartlek session with an odd number of legs that comprise uphill, downhill and level running. This will train all the aspects of your running in one go. Treat the first leg as effort, the next as recovery and then the following as effort once again. If it's a three-leg fartlek then the first leg will become a recovery leg on the second circuit thus ensuring a mix in the training benefits.

Distances

With all three of these types of session, a variety of distances can and should be used.

Short hills of between 30 and 60 seconds running time can be used to develop strength and power. For these short distances it is possible to attack the incline and make the session very intensive without an undue amount of fatigue setting in.

These short sessions will also help you to experiment with and develop your arm movement. This type of session would normally entail 3 sets of 8 to 10 reps with an easy jog/walk back down as the recovery. Recovery between the sets would be a 5 to 7 minute easy recovery run.

Medium hills of between 2 to 5 minutes will help develop stamina, and aerobic capacity. A portfolio of different sessions of this type should be built-up representing different running surfaces and angles of climb. Normally sessions of this length of rep will comprise of between 10 to 15 reps with an easy jog/walk back down as the recovery. However, shortening the recovery time by increasing the pace of the jog recovery, can bring an element of lactate tolerance training to these sessions.

Long hills of over 5 minutes can be used to develop stamina, strength, pace judgment and lactate tolerance. The length of these hills should represent the length of the hills that you will encounter in your style of race. Being practical, the number of reps will be dependant upon the length of the hill that you are using. Keep the session to 60 minutes excluding warm-up and warm-down and perform as many reps that will fit into the 60 minutes.

Rolling hills can be incorporated into a long and/or steady run. Plan the route to take in hills of a similar length and type that you wish to train on and then treat the climbs as you would during an uphill session.

As always, don't forget to factor into your training the terrain. As stated above, build-up a portfolio of different sessions that will reflect different angles of climb and types of running surface. During a general training phase these sessions can be performed on a rotational basis to build-up overall skill and conditioning. When training moves into a more specific phase aimed at a particular race then the emphasis will move towards those sessions that will mirror the climbs that will be met during the target race.

4.3 So which type of sessions are suitable for which type of off-road running

The table overleaf details the various off-road disciplines and relevant uphill sessions that are appropriate.

Event	Normal Length of Climb	Ascent	Appropriate Type of Uphill Session
Cross-Country	Upto 400 metres. Rarely longer.	Upto 300 ft / 90 metres in one climb.	Short hills and Medium hills upto 3 minutes running time either as reps or fartlek.
Orienteering	Upto 1,000 metres. Rarely longer.	Upto 600 ft / 180 metres in one climb.	Short hills and Medium hills either as reps or fartlek.
Short Trail Races (upto 10 miles/16 kms)	Upto 1 mile/1.5 km and there may be more than one climb.	Upto 1000 ft / 300 metres in one climb.	Short hills and Medium hills either as reps or fartlek. Long hills as reps. Rolling hills as part of a weekend long run of upto 15 miles / 24 kms.
Short Fell Races (upto 6 miles/10 kms)	Upto 3 miles/5 kms. Normally only one climb but may be more.	Upto 2000 ft / 600 metres in one climb.	Short hills and Medium hills either as reps or fartlek. Long hills as reps. Rolling hills as part of a weekend long run of upto 10 miles / 16 kms.
Medium and Long Trail Races (over 10 miles/16 kms)	Upto 2 miles/3 kms and there may be more than one climb.	Upto 1000 ft / 300 metres in one climb but some may go upto 2000 ft / 600 metres.	Short hills and Medium hills either as reps or fartlek. Long hills as reps. Rolling hills as part of a weekend long run of upto 20 miles / 32 kms.

Event	Normal Length of Climb	Ascent	Appropriate Type of Uphill Session
Medium Fell Races (6 to 12 miles / 10 to 19 kms)	Upto 4 miles / 6.4 kms and there may be more than one climb.	Upto 4000 ft / 1200 metres in one climb.	Short hills and Medium hills either as reps or fartlek. Long hills as reps. Rolling hills as part of a weekend long run of upto 15 miles / 24 kms.
Long Fell Races (over 12 miles / 19 kms)	Upto 4 miles /6.4 kms and there will be more than one climb.	Upto 4000 ft / 1200 metres in one climb.	Short hills and Medium hills either as reps or fartlek. Long hills as reps. Rolling hills as part of a weekend long run of upto 20 + miles / 32 + kms.
Mountain Marathons	Upto 4 miles /6.4 kms and there will be more than one climb.	Upto 4000 ft / 1200 metres in one climb.	Medium hills as reps or fartlek. Long hills as reps. Rolling hills as part of a weekend long run of upto 20 + miles / 32 kms including carrying a rucksack.

4.4 Improving your lactate tolerance

The principle of lactate tolerance sessions were explained on page 27.

The typical tolerance improvement session is normally performed with a fast-pace distance run. Around 20 minutes of continuous running at just under 10 k race pace or 80 to 85% of maximum heart rate.

The easiest way of monitoring the amount of effort put into this type of session is by the use of a heart rate monitor. Nowadays they are relatively cheap and easy to use. Even if used for nothing other than this type of session, it is worth investing in one.

This type of session can be done on the roads or for the more committed off-road runner it can be transferred to a more relevant undulating trail or fell setting. However, notice the emphasis on undulating rather than hilly. This will help the continuity of pace without an overdose of lactate affecting the leg muscles. Keeping a constant heart rate over undulating terrain is difficult and will entail changes in the running pace as up and down hill gradients are encountered. The side effect of this is that it can be very useful in developing pace judgement.

Using a heart rate monitor is relatively easy. Every runner has a theoretical maximum heart rate dependent upon age and ability. The instruction booklet with the monitor should be able to show you how to assess yours. For tolerance training you should run with your heart rate in-between 80 and 85 percent of this maximum.

A tolerance improvement session can also utilise a long uphill session where the uphill running is 10 minutes or more. Careful attention needs to be paid to the heart rate in order to ensure that the work level is not exceeded and that the lactate build-up is not excessive. This may entail slowing the pace down as you get further up the hill.

4.5 How often should you do uphill related sessions

As always there is going to be a compromise between what you would like to do and what you can actually fit into a busy week.

Using the four week macrocycle that was introduced in "Downhill Techniques" would give a weekly hill session. This can be mixed as below to give the variety between up, down and terrain training.

A weekly lactate tolerance improvement or threshold session can also be included. While fast-paced, it is not too fast-paced to distract from the weekly long run and can easily be placed as the Saturday session. With Friday as a rest/recovery day from the exertions of the preceding week, this will add balance to the training week.

Use the weekend long run to incorporate rolling hills. These can be either uphill, downhill or both. Instead of rolling hills, it is also possible to include a lactate tolerance session into your long run if you haven't done one the preceding day. Some time after ten miles perform a 20 minute fast paced threshold run. After the twenty minutes, just complete your run as per normal. For a period of time I included this variation into the weekly long run of a sub-3 hour female marathon runner that I was coaching, with quite successful results.

	Week 1	Week 2	Week 3	Week 4
Tuesday Quality Session 1 Hill session	Downhill reps	Uphill reps	Structured fartlek or an up & down session	Terrain training
Thursday Quality Session 2 Speed session	Speed	Speed	Speed	Speed
Saturday	Undulating threshold run	Undulating threshold run	Undulating threshold run	Undulating threshold run
Sunday Weekend Run	Long run including rolling hills	Long run including rolling hills	Long run including rolling hills	Long run including rolling hills

A macrocycle is a training plan over an extended period of time such as shown for a month or four week cycle. A microcycle is a shorter training period which would normally detail seven days or one week.

Not all of us have access to the hills all of the time. When necessary it is perfectly acceptable to perform hill reps on the road.

Putting it all together.

All the different aspects of running uphill from conditioning the body to the different techniques that can be used have been explored. In this last section, we will look at four specific scenarios and putting all the techniques together to see how they look.

The four scenarios are :
1. Shallow climb, good running surface.
2. Medium climb, medium surface.
3. Steep climb, medium surface.
4. Steep climb, rough surface.

5. Summary

Many runners have an aversion to the hills and put up with them as a necessary evil that goes with the joys of off-road running.

You've now read this book, seen how to prepare and use the various tricks of the trade. Hopefully, you'll have even started to put some of them into practice.

Now change the mindset. Hills don't have to become your bosom-buddies but they are nothing to be feared. Prepare for them properly and they can be a valuable weapon in "whooping the ass" of your competitors.

Provided that they haven't read this book as well ……………...

Photo: John Howells

Shallow climb, good running surface.

On a shallow climb with a good running surface it is possible to maintain a normal running action.

Stride length can be normal although if the climb is long, it may be necessary to shorten it a little to help prevent fatigue setting in.

Arm movement would move from the cross-body style to the backwards and forwards movement. How vigorous the movement would be will be dependent upon the length of the hill.

Eyes should be focussed straight in front. Try to resist the urge to keep looking up at the top of the hill. It can be mentally demoralising if the top does not seem to come towards you.

Slightly lean the body forwards and into the hill in order to ensure forward momentum.

Medium climb, medium surface.

Here the angle of the climb is steeper and the surface may be grass, track or path.

Stride length will be shortened due to the increased angle of climb. The amount of shortening will depend on the angle but ensure that the leg muscles feel relaxed. Too long a length will cause the muscles to tighten and tire.

The arm movement would be backwards and forwards with the height of the swing varying dependent upon the length of the climb.

Eyes should be focussed straight in front and looking for any loose surfaces such as stones, etc.

Lean with the body slightly more into the hill than you would with a shallower climb.

Footplant would be on the ball of the foot.

Steep climb, medium surface.

The angle of climb is steep and the surface may be grass, track or path.
The stride length is drastically reduced. With very steep slopes the movement
will resemble walking upstairs. It may be possible to run on shorter hills
although on longer climbs the runner may have to resort to walking.

The arm movement will be backwards and forwards but the height of the swing
will be curtailed. Even when walking ensure that arm movement exists in order
to maintain forward momentum.

Eyes should be focussed straight in front and you should be constantly aware of
the running surface as on a steep slope it may suddenly change.

Ensure that the body leans into the hill even when walking. If this is not done,
momentum will be lost.

Footplant will be on the ball of the foot.

Steep climb, rough surface.

The angle of climb is steep and the surface may be rough grass, path or rock.
Because of the steep angle the surface may be loose and possibly slippery.
Unlikely that you will be able to do anything other than walk so the stride length
will be severely reduced. The length may even be shorter than when compared
to a normal walking length.
The arm movement pattern will be difficult to maintain. When necessary the
hands can be used on the legs in order to help take some of the strain away from
the leg muscles. At times it may even be necessary to use the hands to pull you
up.
Eyes will be focussed in front of you and assessing the ground surface.
Lean well into the hill. Resist the urge to stand upright.

About the Author

Kev Shevels is a man who has forgotten more than most about off-road running. Its not that he knew it in the first place, its just that at his age the memory has started to go along with lots of other things such as a slim waistline …………………..

A runner for over thirty years, Kev has been involved in off-road running for over twenty-eight of those years. During this time he has tried his hand at most of the different styles of this discipline, from fell, to trail, to mountain marathons, to ultra-trails, to orienteering, to mountain running. During this time he managed to raise himself up from being a lousy-level runner all the way to the dizzy heights of mediocrity. However, what he did also do is pick up an extensive knowledge and experience of running off-road which he has been able to pass onto others through coaching and encouragement.

A founder member of the Quakers Running Club and Durham Fell Runners, two of the most enthusiastic off-road running clubs in the North East, Kev has been a qualified UK Athletics Level 3 coach for the past nine years, specialising in Fell and Hill Running. Most of his coaching nowadays being done through Durham Fell Runners and the Run Off-Road organisation.

However, to some people his main claim to fame is as a race organiser. Over the last ten years, Kev has organised numerous races, from fell, to trail, to road and cross-country. Some years even organising as many as twenty events which partially explains the lack of training and the fact that he can no longer see his toes.

Yes, at one point the author was a lean, mean running machine. It was in the past but he can still remember !

The Run Off-Road Series

Run Off-Road is the name adopted by Trailguides for it's publications aimed at the fell, hill, trail and mountain runner. This series of books is designed to promote the sport of off-road running in all it's many forms and to encourage the participants to improve and develop their abilities and skills in order to further increase their enjoyment of the sport.

This is an evolving series of books that is constantly expanding. See our website at www.trailguides.co.uk and subscribe to our newsletter for regular updates on our range of publications.

At the time of writing the titles in the series include:

An Introduction to Trail and Fell Running
Downhill Techniques for Off-Road Runners
Uphill Techniques for Off-road Runners
Terrain Training for Off-road Runners
Mountain Marathon Preparation
Navigation for Off-Road Runners
Long and Ultra Distance Off-Road Running

Coming soon
The Mountain Marathon Book

Disclaimer

The information contained in these pages is provided in good faith, but no warranty is made for its accuracy. The contents are, at the time of writing and to the best of my knowledge, up-to-date and correct. However, the world is a changing environment and what is correct one day may not be so the next. The suggested training regimes contained in this publication are exactly that, suggested. It is the reader's responsibility to judge their own level of fitness and whether they are capable of performing any of the said activities.

No guarantee whatsoever is provided by the author and his team and no liability is accepted for any loss, damage or injury of any kind resulting from the use of these pages. Nor as a result of any defect or inaccuracy in them.

As with all outdoor activities, you and you alone are responsible for your safety and well being.